DAY OF INFAMY

The Story of the Attack on Pearl Harbor

BY STEVEN OTFINOSKI

Consultant:
Dennis Showalter, PhD
Professor of History
Colorado College

CAPSTONE PRESS
a capstone imprint

Tangled History is published by Capstone Press,
1710 Roe Crest Drive, North Mankato, Minnesota 56003
www.capstonepub.com

Library of Congress Cataloging-in-Publication Data
Otfinoski, Steven.
Day of infamy : the story of the attack on Pearl Harbor / by Steven Otfinoski.
pages cm. —(Tangled history)
Includes bibliographical references and index.
Summary: "In a narrative nonfiction format, follows people who experienced the
attack on Pearl Harbor"— Provided by publisher.
ISBN 978-1-4914-7078-7 (library binding)
ISBN 978-1-4914-7082-4 (pbk.)
ISBN 978-1-4914-7086-2 (ebook pdf)
1. Pearl Harbor (Hawaii), Attack on, 1941—Juvenile literature. I. Title.
D767.92.O78 2016
940.54'26693—dc23   2015010894

Editorial Credits
Adrian Vigliano, editor; Tracy Davies McCabe, designer; Tracy Cummins, media
researcher; Tori Abraham, production specialist

Photo Credits
AP Photo: 101; Corbis: Bettmann, 30, 37, 90, Kingendai/AFLO/Nippon News, 6;
Getty Images: Keystone-France/Gamma-Keystone, 60, Russell Lee, 99, The LIFE
Picture Collection, 81, Thomas D. Mcavoy/The LIFE Picture Collection, 71; Library of
Congress: 17, 48; Navy.mil: Naval History and Heritage Command Photograph, 38;
Shutterstock: Picsfive, Back Cover, Design Element; U.S. Navy photo: 10, 22, 29, 47, 59,
105, U.S. Naval History and Heritage Command Photograph, 82; Wikimedia: NARA,
Cover, 4, Official U.S. Navy photograph, 72.

TABLE OF CONTENTS

FOREWORD

December 7, 1941, began like any other
Sunday morning on the Hawaiian island of Oahu.
Civilians and American military families quietly
went about their business. Some slept late while
others got ready for church. Much of the U.S.
Navy's Pacific Fleet floated gently in the blue-green

waters at Pearl Harbor on Oahu's southern coast. The fleet, along with hundreds of military airplanes on surrounding airfields, was relatively undefended. World War II raged in Europe but the United States had not joined that fight. Relations between the United States and Japan had become worse in recent years, and some thought the two countries might be heading toward war. But with 4,000 miles between Japan and the Hawaiian islands, no one worried about a Japanese attack. They should have.

Admiral Isoroku Yamamoto, commander in chief of the Imperial Japanese Combined Fleet, had led the effort to devise a simple, bold plan nearly a year before. Japanese warplanes would make a sneak attack on Pearl Harbor and destroy the U.S. fleet. This would give Japan at least six months to execute its master plan to take over a large part of Asia—from China to the islands of the South Pacific—without American interference. Japan's leaders had dreamed of building a colonial empire since at least 1931, when they seized Manchuria in northeastern China. Now, as Japanese forces approached American shores, that dream seemed poised to become a reality.

"SURPRISE LOST"

Japanese admiral Isoroku Yamamoto

Mitsuo Fuchida

Commander Mitsuo Fuchida of the Japanese Imperial Navy grimaced as he gazed down from his cockpit at the cover of clouds below. He had left the flagship aircraft carrier *Akagi* an hour and forty minutes earlier to lead 189 pilots and their planes to their designated targets. They would be approaching their goal soon, but the weather seemed to be working against them.

As the planes approached Oahu, Fuchida grew more tense. Would they be able to see their targets with the clouds so thick? Desperate for information, he flicked on the plane's radio and through the static heard music coming from a local Honolulu radio station. Suddenly the music ended and an announcer came

on with the weather forecast: "partly cloudy …
mostly over the mountains … ceiling 3,500 feet …
visibility good."

Visibility good. That was promising. Then, all
at once, Fuchida saw through his binoculars "a long
white line of breaking surf … directly beneath my
plane. It was the northern shore of Oahu." And
there it was—the blue waters of Pearl Harbor with
its battleships neatly lined up like sitting ducks. He
counted them. Six…seven…eight. But where were the
aircraft carriers? They must be out on maneuvers on
the open sea. He was disappointed but there was no
time to worry about it now.

As he prepared to fire the signal gun for the
attack, Fuchida had a critical decision to make. There
were two scenarios for the attack—"Surprise" or
"Surprise Lost." For "Surprise" Fuchida would fire
one time, indicating the Americans were unaware
of the impending invasion and not prepared. The
torpedo planes would go in first, followed by the
horizontal bombers, and finally the dive bombers. If,
however, the Americans already realized they were
under attack, Fuchida would fire his gun twice for

"Surprise Lost." Then the dive bombers and fighters would immediately fire on the island's airfields and antiaircraft ground defenses to halt any resistance. After that, the torpedo planes would come in to attack the ships.

But Fuchida had no idea if the Americans were already aware of their arrival. Reconnaissance planes sent ahead were supposed to send him a report, but he had heard nothing. Time was running out. He had to decide one way or the other. He chose "Surprise" and fired his gun once. The so-called "black dragon" of smoke shot through the air. The dive bombers began to circle, but there was no movement from the fighter planes. Had they not seen the signal? Fuchida fired the gun again. This time the fighters did see it, but unfortunately, so did the dive bombers and other planes. They took it for two shots, signaling "Surprise Lost." The plan was already coming apart as all of the planes prepared to attack at the same moment. It didn't matter, Fuchida decided.

The attack had begun.

"WE'RE UNDER ATTACK"

2

Ford Island lies in the middle of Pearl Harbor.

John William Finn

Chief Petty Officer John William Finn was lying awake in bed when he heard the planes.

It was a sound that Finn, stationed at the Kaneohe Bay Naval Air Station, 12 miles from Pearl Harbor, was familiar with. But not on a Sunday morning, a time to sleep late and rest. He shifted his body and looked at his wife, Alice. She was standing at the bedroom window, gazing out at nearby Hawaiialoh Hill. "Oh John, it's beautiful!" she said. Finn looked up and saw an airplane whiz by against the blue canvas of sky. Then he heard the sound of machine gun fire.

He assumed someone was firing down at the machine gun range.

But why on a Sunday morning? And why are the guns firing so slow? Finn wondered. Another plane flashed by the window.

"Hey, those are aircraft carrier planes," he said to Alice. Was the base holding a mock attack? On a Sunday morning? Just then there was a sharp rap on the apartment door. "My gut had turned to a little lead ball," Finn recalled years later. "I knew something was wrong."

Finn threw on a pair of dungarees and ran for the door. It was his neighbor, Lou Sullivan, the wife of Eddie Sullivan, the next senior ordnance man in his squadron.

"What's up, Lou?" he asked.

"They want you down at the hangar right away," she said.

Finn went back to the bedroom and quickly finished dressing.

"Where are you going?" Alice asked.

"Over to the hangar."

Alice's eyes grew wide. "At this hour?" she said. "On a Sunday?"

"They need me to check something out," he said.

He decided not to tell her that the base might be under attack. He didn't want to alarm her and was hoping against hope that he was wrong.

He put on his shoes and gave her a peck on the cheek. "I'll be back as soon as I can," he said.

"Bill—" she started, but he cut her off.

"It's all right," he said. "Go back to bed. I'll be back soon."

Then before she could say another word, he was out the door.

All was quiet on the USS *Arizona*, one of eight battleships stationed along what was known as Pearl Harbor's Battleship Row. Lieutenant Commander Samuel Glenn Fuqua, 42, one of the ship's senior officers, was eating breakfast in the wardroom. This was one of Fuqua's favorite times of the week. He could sit and linger over a second cup of coffee and read the Sunday newspapers. It was quiet because most of the nearly 1,500 sailors on board were still enjoying a late morning sleep. Those men lucky enough to be off-duty were getting ready to go ashore for a carefree day in Honolulu.

All at once the silence was broken by a short signal on the air raid alarm. Fuqua knew instantly it could mean only one thing. He dropped his paper, grabbed a nearby phone and called the officer of the deck.

His order was short and swift. "Sound general quarters," he said.

Within moments a voice came over the loudspeakers. "This is no drill. This is no drill. General quarters. All hands. General quarters. We're under attack. This is no drill."

As others listened stunned, Fuqua rushed up to the starboard side of the ship's quarterdeck. As he clambered out of the wardroom hatch he looked up and saw a plane zoom by, guns ablaze. He saw the red sun of the Japanese flag painted on its side. The plane was flying about 100 feet above the *Arizona*. Fuqua started to run forward on the quarterdeck. As he reached the starboard gangway, a flash blinded him and the ship was rocked by a tremendous explosion. Fuqua felt himself being lifted upward and then came down onto the hard deck with terrific force. Darkness enveloped him.

Mitsuo Fuchida

Having watched the other bombers go into action, Commander Fuchida prepared to drop some bombs himself. At an altitude of 9,843 feet (3,000 meters), he prepared to make a run. If the Americans were initially taken by surprise, a few of them were now beginning to fight back.

"Suddenly my plane bounced as if struck by a club," Fuchida later recalled. Antiaircraft fire had struck his plane. He turned to assess the damage.

"The fuselage is holed and the rudder wire damaged," said the radioman seated behind him.

Fuchida had lost his focus and feared they had overshot the target. He circled around to have another try. Suddenly the plane shook again. This time it wasn't American fire from the ground but an explosion of tremendous proportions. Fuchida saw "a huge column of dark red smoke" rising into the atmosphere. It was the USS *Arizona* being hit several miles away in Pearl Harbor, although Fuchida didn't know it at the time. What he did know was that the fleet had been seriously damaged. Exhilarated, he joined the next bombing run over the harbor. Fuchida lay down on the cockpit floor and slid open a peephole. He followed the path of four bombs until they disappeared from sight far below. He waited until two small puffs of smoke rose into the air. "Two hits!" he cried.

Elizabeth McIntosh

Elizabeth McIntosh, like most civilians on Oahu, was enjoying the ease of a Sunday morning. At age 26, McIntosh was a part-time reporter for the *Honolulu Star-Bulletin*. Sunday was usually a slow news day, and McIntosh planned to enjoy it. Right now she was listening to a radio concert by the famed Mormon Tabernacle Choir. Suddenly the music was interrupted by the urgent voice of an announcer. "The islands are under attack," he said. "This is the real McCoy."

McIntosh was concerned, but when the music started again she thought to herself, "Oh, this is just another Army maneuver or something,"

A short time later, the phone rang. It was one of the paper's photographers, with whom she had worked many times. "Hey," he said, "something's happened. We've gotta get down, and I've got to cover it and you see what you can do."

McIntosh grabbed her notepad and pen and waited for his arrival. The photographer pulled up in front of her house and then the two of them took off.

The drive to downtown Honolulu was about 10 miles. They drove past quiet streets where they saw people strolling to church wearing their Sunday best. Other people were out walking their dogs. No one looked worried.

"We can't be under attack," McIntosh said. "Everything's normal. It can't be true."

Sixteen-year-old John Garcia was in the middle of a pleasant dream when he felt someone shaking him.

"Wake up, John! Wake up!" It was his grandmother.

"What is it?" he said, yawning.

"The man on the radio says the island is under attack."

Garcia shook his sleepy head. "No, they're just practicing," he said, rolling over in bed.

"No, no," insisted his grandmother. "It's an attack. The man said all Pearl Harbor workers are to report to work. Now."

John sighed. Attack or no attack, he had his orders. As an apprentice pipe fitter at the Pearl Harbor Navy yard he was obliged to show up. Garcia, a native Hawaiian, was proud to be working for the U.S. Navy, but not on a Sunday morning.

Still skeptical about an attack, he pulled on a bathrobe and padded out to the front porch. He looked up and saw fighter planes spitting bullets. From the ground, antiaircraft guns were returning the fire.

"Oh boy," he said. He quickly threw on some clothes and hopped on his motorcycle for the 10-minute ride to the Navy yard.

"THE SHIP WAS A MASS OF FLAMES"

3

John William Finn

John Finn hopped into his 1938 black Ford sedan and turned on the ignition. As he did, Eddie Sullivan, known as "Sully," came running. He was buttoning his shirt over his belly and puffing on a cigarette. He jumped into the car and they took off. The naval station was only a mile away, and Finn drove at 20 miles per hour, the official base speed. He wasn't going to panic and have an accident.

At age 32 Finn was a 15-year Navy veteran. The son of a Los Angeles plumber, he had dropped out of school at age 14 and joined the Navy three years later. The young enlisted men called him "the Old Chief." He knew they meant it as a mark of respect, even if sometimes they said it with a grin on their faces.

23

As he drove Finn heard a plane roar overhead. Looking up he saw the pilot do a wingover, climbing steeply into the sky and then dropping sharply, leveling off in the opposite direction. And there on the underside of the wing was what the soldiers called the "big old red meatball"—the official insignia of Japan—the rising sun. Finn threw the Ford into second gear and stepped on the gas.

Samuel Glenn Fuqua

USS *Arizona*, 8:12 a.m.

Lt. Commander Fuqua didn't know how long he had been unconscious, but when he came to he beheld a scene of pure horror. The ship was a mass of flames. Fuqua wondered if the *Arizona's* forward magazine, which held 50 tons of gunpowder and ammunition, had exploded. Looking around he could see that many men were either dead or dying from their injuries. The fortunate ones were stumbling up onto the quarterdeck from below, some burned, some seriously injured, and some merely stunned. Feeling his arms and legs, Fuqua was grateful to be in this last group.

Fuqua saw that someone had cut the *Arizona* free from the repair ship USS *Vestal* to which it was anchored. The damaged *Vestal* managed to move up the harbor. But the much larger *Arizona*, seriously wounded and possibly sinking, remained an easy target for the Japanese bombers.

Fuqua went into action. The men were dazed and frightened, so he had to remain cool and calm. He had to set an example. It was the only way he was going to get them off the ship alive.

He ordered the men around the nearest turrets to turn on the fire mains to quench the flames shooting up from the boat deck. They tried to do as he said but quickly found there was no water. After a quick search, the men found some CO_2 tanks on the port side of the ship and sprayed the fire. There was no way they could put out the inferno, but at least they could prevent the flames from immediately reaching the quarterdeck. This allowed them to rescue the men—some of whom were on fire—running down the boat deck.

Fuqua saw that oil leaking from the ship had ignited on the water. Some of the men had left the ship on lifeboats, but these boats were headed for the burning waters and the men were forced to abandon them. However, the admiral's barge, a good-sized motorboat used by officers for harbor transport, was still on deck and a number of men were trying to release it. Meanwhile, Fuqua sent two ensigns belowdecks to find the senior officers—Rear Admiral Isaac Kidd and Captain Franklin Van Valkenburgh. When they reached the men's cabins, the ensigns were wading knee-deep in water. The *Arizona* was quickly sinking. They reported back that they couldn't find either officer. Fuqua came to the grim conclusion that at the time of the explosion the two officers had been on the bridge and must have been instantly killed. He had to assume he was the senior officer now.

When John Finn reached the hangars at the air station he found most of the seaplanes on the ground already damaged or destroyed by the Japanese bombers. Men were running around the field, some trying to save the planes, others running for safety.

Finn ran into a hangar and found that there were carts containing 500-pound (227-kilogram) TNT depth charges. If a bullet struck one of these it would blow the hangar to pieces. Finn decided he had to fight back and try to keep the Japanese from bombing the hangars. He looked for a gun mount but found none. A month earlier he had asked his superiors to allow him to build some gun mounts for machine guns for land-based shooting and had gotten no response.

Finn found one of his radiomen near the

door to the hangar firing a .30 caliber machine gun placed on a makeshift mount. Realizing the only thing that the man might hit was one of his own men on the ground near the hangar, Finn ordered him to move it out into the open where the Japanese planes were flying overhead. "We can't, Chief," he replied. "They're firing at us!" Without another word, Finn grabbed the mounted gun and dragged it 20 yards out toward the runway. From here, he would have a good view of the planes overhead. By the same token, they would have a clear view of him.

Not thinking of the consequences, Finn pushed up the gun's barrel, put his finger on the trigger, and began firing as more Japanese planes came into sight.

Sailors at Kaneohe Bay Naval Air Station tried to save
planes that were damaged on the ground.

"NO DRILL"

4

Franklin Roosevelt began collecting stamps when he was eight years old.

Franklin Delano Roosevelt

It was a leisurely Sunday in the nation's capital. President Franklin Delano Roosevelt was upstairs in his spacious White House study, enjoying a talk with his old friend and closest advisor, Harry Hopkins. Roosevelt's wife, First Lady Eleanor Roosevelt, was serving lunch to 31 guests downstairs.

Roosevelt preferred doing business in his study rather than downstairs in the Oval Office. He affectionately called it "the Oval Study." Earlier in the day Roosevelt had met with the Chinese ambassador, who voiced concern about Japanese aggression against his country. He assured the ambassador that the United States would defend China from the Japanese if necessary.

Roosevelt continued to worry about the militaristic leadership of Japanese prime minister Tojo. In recent years Japan had occupied parts of

China and seemed poised to seize European colonies in Southeast Asia. Roosevelt knew that Secretary of State Cordell Hull was in the midst of negotiations with Japanese ambassadors, trying to work out a peaceful resolution, but the outlook wasn't promising.

After the meeting with the Chinese ambassador, Roosevelt and Hopkins had lunch in the study. Now, his little Scottish terrier Fala in his lap, Roosevelt tried to relax by poring over his massive stamp collection. Hopkins, who was 71 and in poor health, rested on the sofa. Then the phone rang.

The operator put through Secretary of the Navy Frank Knox. "Mr. President," said Knox, "we've picked up a radio from Honolulu from the commander-in-chief of our forces there advising all our stations that an air raid attack was on and that it was 'no drill.' It looks as if the Japanese have attacked Pearl Harbor."

"No!" Roosevelt gasped, feeling the word catch in his throat as he sat up straight in his chair. He hoped that somehow the message was a mistake, but the sinking feeling in his gut told him otherwise.

Hopkins shook his head, refusing to believe the

news. But Roosevelt immediately called Secretary of War Henry Stimson. After that he called Secretary of State Hull, who was about to receive two Japanese ambassadors at his Washington office. Roosevelt told Hull the news and ordered him not to say anything about the attack to the ambassadors. "Cordell," said Roosevelt, "bow them out."

Collecting his thoughts, the president also rang up his personal secretary, Grace Tully, and his son, Marine Captain James Roosevelt. Roosevelt ordered them all to come directly to the White House. *He knew it was going to be a long day.*

John Garcia arrived at the naval yard to find Battleship Row in turmoil. The USS *Shaw*, the ship he had been working on, was on fire from the bombing. Garcia went to retrieve his toolbox in the pipe fitter's shop when a swarm of Japanese planes swooped down for another attack. Garcia ran for cover under a set of concrete steps in dry dock near the battleship USS *Pennsylvania*.

As he sat there listening to the gunfire from the planes overhead, a red-faced officer crouched down next to him. "We have to get those fires out," the officer said. "Get onto that ship and see what you can do." Garcia knew that the ship's magazines were several decks below on the *Pennsylvania*. Once the fire reached them, there would be a massive explosion, much like the one that had already occurred on the USS *Arizona*. Anyone going on board ran the risk of being blown to bits at any moment. Garcia wanted to help, but he wasn't foolhardy. He shook his head. "There [isn't any] way I'm gonna go down there," he told the officer.

The officer's eyes widened as his face grew redder. Garcia thought the man might throttle him. "What's your name?" the officer said sharply.

Feeling he was in the right to refuse the officer's command, Garcia didn't lie.

"John Garcia," he said.

"I'll remember that name," said the officer as he rushed off.

Garcia remained where he was, waiting for the firing to stop so he could get to his toolbox.

Elizabeth McIntosh

As Elizabeth McIntosh and her photographer drew closer to the heart of the city, the landscape changed. They began to see signs of the bombing—people walking around dazed, buildings damaged or destroyed. It felt like a war zone. Were the Japanese targeting the entire island or hitting civilian targets by accident? They had no way of knowing, but could only assume the worst. Soon they stopped in front of a wrecked site that had once been an open-air market. McIntosh couldn't believe her eyes. There, sitting in the midst of the wreckage of Christmas decorations, was a small boy playing with a toy.

"There's a picture for you," she said.

The photographer looked at the boy and shook his head.

"It's no good," he said. "Hey, the kid looks just too happy. Do something about it."

McIntosh looked at him, puzzled. The photographer moved his thumb and forefinger together in a pinching gesture. McIntosh got the message. Feeling slightly guilty, she approached the boy and pinched him sharply on the arm. He looked up at her, startled, and then began to cry.

"That's it!" cried the photographer and snapped half a dozen pictures.

Afterward, McIntosh wondered why the boy was alone and what had happened to his mother and father.

Residents of Honolulu were shocked at the damage to the city.

"WE'RE ALL IN THE SAME BOAT NOW"

5

The USS *Shaw* exploded when raging fires reached the ship's forward magazine.

John Garcia

John Garcia felt bad. He wanted to help, but he didn't want to die either. He was no hero, just a 16-year-old Hawaiian kid working for the Navy for 62 cents an hour. Then another officer came up to him and asked for help. He wanted Garcia to go into the harbor waters and retrieve sailors who had been blown off their ships by the bomb and torpedo explosions. Garcia agreed to do it. He knew it would be dangerous, but saving wounded sailors seemed less suicidal than working on a ship that was about to explode.

The Japanese planes had left, at least for the moment. There were no more explosions, although the ships continued to burn. Garcia stripped down to his underwear and entered the chilly waters of the harbor. Near the USS *Pennsylvania* he found a sailor floating in the water, face up. Garcia prayed that the man was still alive. He was. The sailor stared up gratefully as Garcia placed one hand under his chin and began to swim to shore, pulling him behind. On land, the young man lifted the sailor up and laid him out on the ground. Gasping for air, the sailor looked at him, smiled, and whispered hoarsely, "Thanks, pal." Medics came and took the man away. Feeling relieved that the sailor had survived, Garcia wiped his face, turned, and reentered the water.

Mitsuo Fuchida

Bomber over Pearl Harbor, 8:54 a.m.

After the first attack ended, there was a brief lull as the Japanese regrouped. Flight Commander Fuchida waited anxiously in his cockpit for the second wave of planes to attack. And here they came, right on schedule. Fuchida expected that this time his planes would be less effective. Smoke from the burning ships made visibility difficult for the Japanese pilots. They couldn't see their targets. Also, the Americans were now beginning to respond to the attack with antiaircraft weapons on the ground and fighter planes in the air.

As for the Japanese pilots, they looked for new targets to hit. Fuchida saw that the destruction they were wreaking was terrible, but he knew it was necessary if Japan was to fulfill its destiny.

Samuel Glenn Fuqua

Aboard the USS *Arizona*, 8:57 a.m.

Lt. Commander Fuqua was doing his best to keep the men moving as the flames on the USS *Arizona* burned higher. He ordered the able bodied to help the wounded into the admiral's barge for the short but challenging quarter-mile journey to Ford Island. His cool demeanor seemed to rub off on the men around him. They moved quickly, with purpose, without panicking.

The admiral's barge was nearly filled, but Fuqua refused to get aboard until he knew everyone else was off the *Arizona*. One of the last to leave was sailor Jim Lawson. Another sailor, eyes filled with terror, stuck to Lawson like a burr. "Guns," he said, using Lawson's nickname, "I can't swim."

Fearing the barge wouldn't leave the *Arizona* in time, Lawson decided to take to the water. "Well, we gotta go," he said, pushing his friend over the side. Then he jumped in right behind him.

Fuqua watched them, hoping they'd make it to shore. He felt confident that all the men who could be helped were off the *Arizona*. Knowing nothing more could be done, he climbed into the barge and gave the order to lower it.

Franklin Delano Roosevelt
The White House, 8:58 a.m. (2:28 p.m. EST)

News from Pearl Harbor came in dribs and drabs to Roosevelt's Oval Study, and each report felt more distressing than the last. Since there was no direct line between the White House and Pearl Harbor, the president had to rely on his secretary, Grace Tully. She had been taking messages from Chief of Naval Operations Harold Stark, then transcribing them in Roosevelt's bedroom, which served as her temporary office. Finally she brought the typed reports down the hall for him to read.

While waiting for Tully's reports, Roosevelt met with Stephen Early, the White House's first full-time press secretary. The president dictated a message to Early. At 2:30 p.m., Early delivered the message to the three major wire services in a conference hookup. Roosevelt listened, heavy hearted, as Early spoke to the media:

"At 7:55 a.m., Hawaiian time, the Japanese bombed Pearl Harbor. The attacks are continuing and ... no, I don't know how many are dead."

Later in the afternoon a call came through from British prime minister Winston Churchill and U.S. ambassador John Winant. "Mr. President, what's this about Japan?" was Churchill's first question.

To Roosevelt, Churchill sounded both sad and relieved. For well over a year he had been trying to persuade the president to join Great Britain in the war against Germany and Italy. Now he must be thinking that the United States would be forced to join the fight.

"It's quite true," said Roosevelt. "They have attacked us at Pearl Harbor. We are all in the same boat now."

Slowly the barge pulled away from the burning hulk that had once been the proud battleship USS *Arizona*. Lt. Commander Fuqua, at the wheel, felt bad for the ship and the many men, dead or dying, who were going down with it. Their numbers had to be in the hundreds, maybe more. But Fuqua tried to put them out of his mind and focus on the living. Many battered men stood around him on deck while others floated or swam in the oil-slick, smoky waters beside the barge.

Fuqua told the men to pull aboard any sailors they spotted in the water. He saw Jim Lawson only a few feet from the craft, struggling to stay afloat. He didn't see the other sailor who had jumped from the *Arizona* with Lawson. Fuqua grabbed Lawson and pulled him onto the barge. Lawson flashed a weary grin and pointed to another figure thrashing in the black waters. It was the sailor who said he couldn't swim. Lawson then tied a T-shirt around his own ankle, and handed the other end of the shirt to the sailor in the water. The man held on and the barge towed him through the water.

Ford Island lay less than a quarter of a mile away, but it seemed much farther. Resisting the urge to open the engine's throttle, Fuqua kept the barge moving slowly so they could pick up as many men in the water as possible.

He gripped the wheel, praying that they'd all make it to shore in one piece.

John William Finn

It had been nearly an hour since John Finn began firing at the Japanese planes. He didn't know for certain if he had brought down a single plane in all that time. At least it felt good to be fighting back, to let the enemy know that they weren't just sitting there and taking it. Other men were running around the station, some trying to move planes out of harm's way and others firing back with whatever weapons they could find.

Finn hardly noticed the men around him, so intent was he on his shooting. He also paid as little attention as possible to the shrapnel and bullets that had hit him. He had been struck many times, including in the left arm, left foot, right elbow, and right thumb. His scalp had been cut neatly by flying metal and his chest felt as if a number of bones had been broken. He tried to ignore the pain.

From somewhere nearby he thought he heard one of the young sailors in his crew cry out: "The old chief had the top of his head knocked off!"

Finn smiled. It was just like them to exaggerate. At that moment he felt a sharp pain in his arm as another piece of shrapnel pierced his body. He clenched his jaw and set his sights on the bombers circling above.

Gun crews did their best to protect themselves as they tried to mount a defense against attacking planes.

"I COUNT FOUR BATTLESHIPS DEFINITELY SUNK..."

6

The USS *Arizona* was engulfed in flames and smoke before sinking.

Samuel Glenn Fuqua

Waters of Pearl Harbor off Ford Island,
9:15 a.m.

The admiral's barge was filling up quickly. More than 60 men were aboard now. Some feared the vessel might sink or capsize under the growing weight and that they wouldn't make it to Ford Island, now only a tantalizing few hundred yards away. But Lt. Commander Fuqua was determined to pick up every remaining man in the water along the way.

Many of the men they pulled aboard, like Lawson, were coated with oil that glistened on their skin in the morning sun. It would take them days of scrubbing to get all the oil off.

Some of the men looked aft to see the USS *Arizona* as she sank to the bottom of the harbor, still burning. Fuqua didn't look back, but kept his eyes trained on the waters around the barge and the island ahead.

The closer they got to the island, the louder the gunfire seemed to rain down around them. It was as if the Japanese pilots were determined to stop them before they reached land.

The boat was nearly full now with about 70 men. Fuqua opened the throttle as they neared the island.

"We're going to make it," Lawson said hoarsely.
Fuqua patted him on the shoulder, too overcome with emotion to speak. Suddenly all of his feelings were rising to the surface, like the oil that covered the water. He swallowed hard and then told a few men around him to prepare the barge for landing.

John Finn tried to take advantage of the lulls when the planes went away. He knew the bomb-handling carts in the hangars were still a hazard. Rushing over to the hangars, he told Sully to take the carts out in the squadron truck.

"Where shall I take 'em?" Sully asked.

"Take 'em out and disperse 'em in the brush," Finn replied. "Whatever you do, don't put them all in one place." Then he went back to the machine gun.

During another lull, Finn returned to the hangars and saw that none of the carts had been moved. Had Sully lost his nerve and run off? He fumed as he thought about it.

But Finn had been wrong. A while later, Sully drove up in the squadron truck. "I had a hard time tracking it down," he explained.

But now he needed a tractor to open the heavy doors wide enough to get the carts out. He got the tractor, opened the doors, and finally used the truck to tow the carts far from the hangar.

As Sully drove away, Finn rushed back to his machine gun just as another formation of Japanese planes came into view.

Samuel Glenn Fuqua

Ford Island, 9:25 a.m.

As soon as the barge hit the shore, sailors scrambled out and onto the ground, some limping, some holding onto injured arms and sides. They were all grateful to be alive and anxious to get away from the buzzing Japanese bombers. A badly burned man who looked more dead than alive welcomed them.

The man opened his arms pitifully and begged the arriving men for help. For once, Lt. Commander Fuqua could do nothing. The man, even if he was rushed immediately to a hospital, was beyond help.

Fuqua wanted to wrap his arms around the poor soul and comfort him, but there wasn't time. He had to get his men to shelter as quickly as possible.

As Fuqua looked up the beach, he saw Marines rushing toward them. They said they would bring the new arrivals to a safe haven. Fuqua joined them, overcome with gratitude to have made it this far.

Franklin Delano Roosevelt
The White House, 9:30 a.m. (3:00 p.m. EST)

The news from Pearl Harbor was taking on a dreadful shape. Fuzzy data and hazy rumors were solidifying into hard facts. And the facts were devastating. Many ships were destroyed or badly damaged. The number of military and civilian casualties was still being tallied, but it was in the hundreds, if not thousands. Roosevelt wondered if the Japanese would follow the sneak attack with a major invasion of the Hawaiian Islands. Even more grim was the thought of a strike on the west coast of the United States.

The president convened his war council in the Oval Study. The group consisted of Harry Hopkins, Secretary of State Hull, Secretary of War Stimson, Navy Secretary Knox, General George Marshall of the Army, and Admiral Harold Stark.

As members of the council began to express their outrage, shock, and frustration, Roosevelt listened, trying to remain calm and deliberate. Despite his own frustration and the exhaustion of the day, he did everything he could to hold his emotions in check. But deep down a part of him felt almost relieved.

For months Roosevelt had struggled with the decision of whether to enter the war or stay out of it.

He had given what support he could to Great Britain. He had sold, loaned, or leased war materials to the British, including 50 destroyers. And Britain also had the support of Commonwealth Allies such as Australia and Canada. But since the fall of France, Roosevelt knew the British fight against Nazi Germany had become increasingly lonely. Now it seemed that the Japanese had made the decision for the president. There was no turning back.

With the help of the war council, Roosevelt planned two evening meetings—the first with his full cabinet and the second with congressional leaders. The group also decided that the president would deliver a formal address the next day to a joint session of Congress that would be broadcast on radio to the nation. He would lay out what happened at Pearl Harbor and ask Congress for a declaration of war against Japan. Roosevelt didn't feel ready to declare war on Germany, but told the group his belief that Nazi dictator Adolf Hitler would declare war on the United States.

Alone after the meeting, Roosevelt began to plan his address. Though he had a staff of able speechwriters, they were all out of town, caught off-guard by the attack. He would have to write this speech, one he knew might be the most important of his presidency, by himself.

As the second attack wound down, Commander Fuchida watched one warplane after another circle and head back to the aircraft carriers that had brought them here from Japan. He circled his plane around to survey their handiwork. One by one, he noted aloud the ships damaged or destroyed.

"I count four battleships definitely sunk, and three severely damaged and extensive damage has also been inflicted upon other types of ships." He lingered a little longer over the devastation and then veered off to the north for the flight back to the carrier.

John Garcia

The Japanese planes had gone as abruptly as they had come. The only sounds now were the wails of ambulances, coming and going in the naval yard with depressing regularity. John Garcia was tired. For the past hour he had been in the water, swimming to floating or struggling men and pulling them to safety. As soon as he brought them to land, another worker would lift them into a waiting ambulance to be taken to the hospital. Some of the men he pulled out were alive, eyes closed, gasping for air. Others had their eyes open and didn't move. Garcia knew some of them must be dead.

Garcia wasn't working alone. There were other young men, mostly Hawaiians, involved in the rescue efforts. He felt good, almost proud, that his people were helping during this awful tragedy.

Garcia's thoughts turned to his girlfriend of three years, who lived only a few blocks from his house. He wished he had stopped to see her before he went to the yard. She would have been getting ready for church when the bombs fell. He knew she was safe. After all, the Japanese had targeted the battleships in the harbor and the airplanes on the ground, not civilian homes. He still wished he could be with her, to comfort her. But he couldn't leave. Just then he spotted another sailor floating in the water.

He dove in immediately, hoping that the man was still alive.

Sailors tried to focus on doing whatever they could to help, even as the chaos of the attack continued.

"...A DATE WHICH WHICH WILL LIVE IN INFAMY"

The second attack looked like it was over, but John Finn wasn't taking any chances. He stayed at his post on the runway. Before long he noticed a little black speck in the sky. At first he thought it was a seagull, but as it drew closer he could clearly see it was a lone Japanese plane.

He began firing his machine gun, and then realized the plane was still several miles away and he was wasting ammunition. He lost sight of the plane for a time in the smoke rising from the burning planes on the ground. When the plane emerged from the smoke, it seemed to be headed straight for him. Finn fired several rounds before the plane zoomed over his head. When he whirled around it had disappeared behind some nearby buildings.

"There's no way in the world that I could have missed him," he muttered.

Roosevelt called Grace Tully into the Oval Study. "Sit down, Grace," he said. "I'm going before Congress tomorrow. I'd like to dictate my message. It will be short."

She gave a weary smile and sat down, taking out her notebook. Roosevelt knew how hard she had been working all afternoon. The typed reports she had brought him were stacked up all around on the desk, along with the notes for his speech.

But as he dictated he found he didn't need to refer to a single note he had written. When he finished, Tully typed up the draft. Alone again, he read it over, revising a word here or there.

While reading he kept returning to the first sentence. Something about it bothered him. "Yesterday, December seventh, 1941," he read, "a date which will live in world history ... " He knew he would have to be more emphatic to convince the nation to follow him into a terrible war they had been avoiding for more than two years. He crossed out "world history" and wrote "infamy."

"A date which will live in infamy," he read, feeling more satisfied.

Edward R. Murrow
The White House, 11:30 a.m. (5:00 p.m. EST)

CBS news correspondent Edward Murrow looked at his wife, Janet, as they sat enjoying a meal hosted by the First Lady. They were part of a small group of guests, all of whom, Murrow assumed, must be a bit surprised that the dinner was still on despite the terrible news from Hawaii. Though the meal had not been canceled, President Roosevelt was unable to attend. Mrs. Roosevelt told them that her husband was meeting with congressional and military leaders.

Murrow had just returned from London, where he had delivered memorable reports back to America from that war-torn city, under attack from German bombers. Now back in the United States for some rest, Murrow found himself a well-known national figure due to his eyewitness reporting.

As Murrow turned his attention back to the meal, an usher approached. The usher brought a message from the president, asking Murrow to stay at the White House after dinner for an informal meeting.

When they finished eating, Janet left for another party. Murrow made his way upstairs. He found a bench outside the president's study and sat down, waiting to be summoned.

Mitsuo Fuchida

Aboard the Japanese aircraft carrier *Akagi*, 1:00 p.m.

Commander Fuchida was the last pilot to land his plane on the carrier. The pilots and the sailors aboard were in a jubilant mood. They had smashed the U.S. Pacific Fleet at Pearl Harbor and had lost very few planes in the process. But Fuchida felt they had not done enough.

When Fuchida met Fleet Commander Vice Admiral Chuichi Nagumo and other officers on the bridge, a heated argument developed. Fuchida listened as several of his superior officers argued strenuously for going back to finish the job they had begun. They pointed out that there were sites they had left untouched that were vital to the Americans. For example, they had not destroyed the tank farms which contained millions of barrels of oil to provide fuel for the fleet. Then there were the missing U.S. carriers that might return soon and be open to attack. And, they reasoned, the Americans would immediately begin to repair the battleships that had not been completely destroyed. If the Japanese returned and destroyed their ship-repair facilities the Americans could not put these ships back into action for a much longer time.

Nagumo listened to the arguments quietly. Then Rear Admiral Ryunosuke Kusaka turned to Nagumo. "The attack is terminated," he said. "We are withdrawing."

"Please do," replied Nagumo.

A good soldier, Fuchida accepted his superiors' decision, although he disagreed with it. He worried the Americans would quickly repair the damage the Japanese planes had done. Then they would strike back with a vengeance. He was sure the only way to avoid that vengeance was for Japan to throw everything it could at the Americans while the opportunity still existed. Fuchida feared what lay ahead for his country.

Elizabeth McIntosh

Elizabeth McIntosh's time on the streets of war-torn Honolulu was brief. Riley Allen, her editor at the *Honolulu Star-Bulletin*, sent her to cover the emergency room of an area hospital.

At the hospital McIntosh found ambulances and firefighters delivering bombing victims, mostly from nearby Hickam Field. Survivors were rushed into the emergency room as doctors worked at a frantic pace. Interns taped windows to prevent shattered glass from flying inside.

The dead were taken to the morgue and put on slabs. Seeing the dead bodies, especially the children, was hard for McIntosh. One dead girl wore a red sweater and clutched a short strand of jump rope in her cold hand. McIntosh was filled with terror and grief at what she saw that day. "I never knew that blood could be so bright red," she wrote in her notebook.

Eleanor Roosevelt

Washington, D.C., 12:40 p.m.
(6:10 p.m. EST)

It was damp and cold outside when First Lady Eleanor Roosevelt left the White House. She was headed for NBC's Washington studios to give her weekly radio address. As she left she saw a sizable crowd gathering outside the White House. The people were bundled in coats and scarves, apparently undeterred by the December cold. They seemed unusually quiet and serious for such a large gathering. *They must be waiting for some official word about the attack from the president,* she thought. As her car pulled away, she heard voices in the crowd begin singing "My Country 'Tis of Thee."

Earlier in the day Eleanor had worked to revise her address in response to the Pearl Harbor attack. Knowing she might be the first public figure to speak to the nation about the events in Hawaii, she wanted to calm fears. She also wanted to assure Americans that the president and the rest of the country's leaders were hard at work, preparing to respond. Looking over her notes again, she hoped that her words would inspire strength and support for her husband's proposals.

Now at the radio studio, Eleanor tried to focus on the speech she was about to give. But she continued to feel the shock of the attack. This very morning at the White House, she had gone briefly into a room where her husband had been meeting with a foreign ambassador. She now felt sure the man had been the Japanese ambassador. He had risen from his seat when she entered the room. *That little man was so polite to me*, she thought, shaking her head. She couldn't seem to get that moment out of her head.

Looking up, she noticed that the young man beside her—an army corporal—seemed nervous. He was scheduled to speak after she finished her address. He seemed to be having trouble opening a clasped book which Eleanor assumed contained his speech. Hoping to reassure the man, she reached over, took the book, and carefully pried the clasp open. The young man took a deep breath as Eleanor smiled and handed back his book.

Feeling more focused now, Eleanor turned to give her address. "I am speaking to you tonight at a very serious moment in our history," she began. She talked about the meetings the president had been holding all day and would continue to hold into the night.

"Whatever is asked of us," she said, "I am sure we can accomplish it. We are the free and unconquerable people of the United States of America."

Roosevelt looked over his cabinet members, gathered around his desk in the Oval Study. They included Secretary of Labor Frances Perkins, the first woman U.S. cabinet member, and Treasury Secretary Henry Morgenthau, both of whom had flown in from New York City to be there.

"My friends," he said, "I believe this may be the most important cabinet meeting since Lincoln convened his cabinet in 1861 during the first days of the Civil War." He then began to explain the specifics of the Japanese attack. He confirmed that Japan had also attacked American-held Guam and Wake Island as well as Hong Kong and Thailand.

He shared the draft of his address with the cabinet. After some discussion he told them he would prepare a longer address for a radio broadcast a few days later that would make the case for war more fully.

Shortly before 9:30 p.m., a buzzer rang. The congressional leaders of both parties had arrived and were waiting for the president.

As news of the attack spread, a crowd began to form outside of the White House.

8

"THEY WERE ALL ASLEEP!"

The presidential study had rarely been so crowded. Cabinet members moved back to make room for the congressional leaders who sat around the president's desk.

Roosevelt spoke quietly. "The casualties, I am sorry to say, were extremely heavy ... "

Senator Tom Connally of Texas, chairman of the Committee on Foreign Relations, broke the somber silence with a question. "How did it happen that our warships were caught like tame ducks in Pearl Harbor?" he asked. "I am amazed at the attack by Japan, but I am still more astounded at what happened to our Navy. They were all asleep! Where were our patrols? They knew these negotiations with the Japanese were going on."

Roosevelt had few answers to Connally's questions. He had been assistant secretary of the Navy under President Woodrow Wilson years earlier and considered himself a Navy man.

He was shocked by the Navy's appparent negligence. But he hadn't asked this group here to debate that issue. He only wanted their consent for his address to a joint session of Congress the next day.

The group eventually agreed and the address was scheduled for 12:30 p.m. Monday. Some asked what Roosevelt was going to say and if it would include a declaration of war, but he put them off. He didn't want to share his speech with the congressional leaders, fearing they would tell others and the word would get out. He needed time, and the nation did too, to digest the terrible events of the past eight hours.

Elizabeth McIntosh
Honolulu, 4:15 p.m.

Emotionally drained from her time in the emergency room, Elizabeth McIntosh was heading home. But first she drove downtown to have another look around. As a reporter, she wanted to get as many details as possible for her story of the attack.

McIntosh visited a drugstore on King Street where she often went after work to have a coke at the soda fountain counter.

The place was a wreck.

Merchandise, burnt by fires set off by the falling bombs, was scattered everywhere. She noticed a Christmas card on the floor, singed by fire, a comic book, and a bicycle blackened by the flames. It seemed strange to her that the soda fountain counter was still intact. On it sat a half-eaten chocolate sundae. McIntosh wondered what happened to the person who had been enjoying it.

Writing frantically, McIntosh filled her notepad. She spied a batch of writing paper on the ground, partly charred by fire and damp from a fire hose. She picked up the paper and jotted down some more notes. Then she looked around one last time and returned to her car.

John Garcia had spent the rest of his day fishing out men from the harbor, and he was exhausted. But his day wasn't over yet. A report had come in that Japanese soldiers had parachuted into Palolo Valley about two miles away. An officer asked him to drive a truckload of marines there to investigate.

When Garcia and the marines arrived they found a house with its lights turned on even though there was an official blackout throughout the island. As Garcia later recalled "The marines started shootin' at that house. The lights went out."

They returned to the naval yard, and Garcia knew he wouldn't be going home that night. All workers were needed and were told to stay at the yard. There was much work to do and no one knew when the Japanese would return. Garcia made himself as comfortable as possible under the concrete steps of the naval yard and tried to get some sleep.

Elizabeth McIntosh

Honolulu, 6:30 p.m.

It was nearly dark when Elizabeth McIntosh arrived home. It seemed like the entire world had fallen apart since she'd left that morning. Once inside, she turned on the radio to get the latest news. A tight-lipped announcer declared that the governor had declared a state of martial law on Oahu. All residents were to turn off their lights, creating a blackout in case the Japanese returned for another attack.

"Stay off the streets," said the announcer, "get your car off the street, do not use the telephone except in cases of extreme emergency, seek shelter, boil all water in case of contamination."

McIntosh shut off all the electric lights and cooked her meager dinner on the stove by the dim glow of a flashlight. She wanted to call her family back in Washington, D.C., to let them know that she was safe, but couldn't justify it as an "extreme emergency." She hoped the ban would be lifted so she could call tomorrow. What would tomorrow bring? More Japanese fighter planes and bombers? Were they going to launch a full invasion and take over the Hawaiian Islands? She'd heard that the Japanese had already launched an invasion in the Philippines.

McIntosh tried to put such thoughts out of her head. She went to bed early, planning to drive to the downtown *Star-Bulletin* offices in the morning to write up her story. Lying in bed, she couldn't stop thinking about the dead girl at the hospital morgue. Finally, she drifted off to the wail of distant ambulances and fire trucks.

Franklin Delano Roosevelt

Roosevelt felt exhausted and emotionally drained, but he knew Edward Murrow had spent the evening waiting patiently outside the study. Hoping it would be his last meeting of the day, he summoned Murrow inside. After greeting one another, the two men were soon joined by William Donovan, leader of the Office of the Coordination of Information. Sandwiches and beer were brought in, and the three of them ate.

Roosevelt had done his best to keep up with Murrow's memorable reporting from London. Now he asked Murrow about the situation in England. He wanted to know how British morale was holding up under the nightly raids of Nazi planes. Murrow praised the spirit of the English and Roosevelt felt his spirits lifting.

When the president described the destruction at Pearl Harbor, he felt his emotions rising to the surface. He told his companions that airplanes were blown up on the airstrips, slamming his fist on the table and crying, "On the ground, by God, on the ground!"

After about half an hour, the three men said their goodbyes. Roosevelt watched them go, wondering what tomorrow would bring.

Many of the airplanes that were bombed on airstrips or in hangars could not be salvaged.

"DADDY WAS KILLED AT HICKAM"

9

Smoke filled the sky as marines watched the attack, awaiting orders.

Franklin Delano Roosevelt

The ringing telephone startled Roosevelt awake. The switchboard operator connected Grace Tully to the president. Tully had just heard from John Winant, the American ambassador in Great Britain. Winant told her that Prime Minister Churchill was planning to ask the British Parliament to declare war against the Japanese.

Roosevelt had Tully dictate a message to Churchill. He asked the prime minister to hold off on the declaration until he'd made his case for war with Congress.

Roosevelt began looking over the morning papers. The pages were filled with news from Hawaii, but the worst news came from naval aide Admiral John Beardell. Beardell reported the latest number of casualties at 1,400 dead and at least another 1,400 injured. Beardell also informed Roosevelt of the sinking of the USS *Arizona*.

Several hours later he began making preparations to dress and prepare for the day. Dressing was a daily ordeal for the president, who had suffered from lower body paralysis since 1921. He relied on help from his personal valet Arthur Prettyman.

As Roosevelt lay in bed, Prettyman helped remove his pajamas, and then slipped metal braces onto the president's legs. Each brace weighed about 5 pounds, and was held in place by three straps. Next Prettyman dressed the president in a black cutaway coat, striped trousers, and a gray and white tie.

At noon Prettyman pushed Roosevelt and his wheelchair to the north portico of the White House. A string of 10 black limousines waited there, along with police officers on motorcycles and Secret Service agents armed with sawed-off shotguns.

The limousine waiting for Roosevelt was not the regular presidential car. Secret Service agent Mike Reilly explained that the Treasury Department had seized the limo from gangster Al Capone. It was the car's protective armored plating that had led Reilly to obtain it from the Treasury Department for the president's ride to the Capitol.

"I hope Mr. Capone doesn't mind," said Roosevelt with a smile.

Roosevelt's son James, a Marine Corps officer, joined his father in the car. Eleanor, wearing a black suit and silver-fox fur, got into a backup car. Then the motorcade made the short drive to Capitol Hill, where the nation's lawmakers were waiting.

Elizabeth McIntosh
Honolulu, 7:00 a.m.

Elizabeth McIntosh hadn't gotten much sleep, but she couldn't stay in bed another minute. There was too much to do. She drove downtown to the offices of the *Honolulu Star-Bulletin* and began writing up her story of the attack.

McIntosh kept getting interrupted in her typing by the phone. Reasoning that someone at the paper could offer them sound advice, women from all over the island were calling in to ask what they could do. Most of the callers were in their homes trying to pick up information from the radio. Many men on the island were out trying to repair the tremendous damage the Japanese left in their wake. The callers had heard rumors that the Japanese were coming back to invade the island. McIntosh could give the callers little comfort.

McIntosh went into Riley Allen's office. He asked her to write a story about the attack from the women's point of view. In light of the calls she had received, it seemed to her a very good idea. Everyone was concerned about the men who had been killed or injured. But what about the women they left behind? How were the women of Honolulu coping with this tremendous tragedy?

John Garcia
Pearl Harbor Naval Yard, 9:30 a.m.

John Garcia had a new assignment. The USS *West Virginia*, one of the seven ships on Battleship Row, had nearly been turned upside down in the attack. It was impossible to reach the men trapped on some of the destroyed battleships, such as the USS *Arizona*, due to raging fires.

However, it was still possible to rescue the men aboard the *West Virginia*. But first workers had to cut through the ship's metal superstructure to get inside.

Garcia grabbed his tools and joined the team of naval yard workers cutting through the ship's hull. Everyone worked as quickly as they could, knowing time was of the essence. No one knew how many men were still alive inside the ship and how long they could live with limited air. The work went on all day.

An officer told Garcia he couldn't go home until the job was finished. He would have to eat and sleep when he could right there in the naval yard. He didn't mind it, but had hoped he could go home that day to see his girlfriend. How he missed her!

Elizabeth McIntosh made the journey around Oahu from Hickam Field to Pearl Harbor and lots of other places in between. She talked to every woman she could find who had a story to tell.

She met a nurse who had barely escaped a rain of bullets at Hickam by dropping to the hospital kitchen floor. She talked with another nurse who had escaped from Pearl Harbor and was collecting paper scraps and pencils for the wounded soldiers in her hospital. The nurse explained that some of the wounded men wanted to write what might be their last messages to loved ones back home. Perhaps the most moving interview was with Theda, a little girl who clutched a big doll in her arms. At one point, Theda leaned over and in a quiet voice said, "Daddy was killed at Hickam."

John William Finn

John Finn did not want to be at the hospital. He had avoided it on Sunday, going instead to sick bay for first aid and then returning to his post. The Japanese attacks had ended, but he stayed to help clean up and do whatever else he could. But this morning his commanding officer insisted that he go to the hospital to be treated for his multiple wounds. Not being one to disobey an order, Finn went to the hospital.

Now Alice was at his bedside, holding his hand and saying soothing words. She was just grateful that he was alive. Finn spied a doctor passing by in the hallway outside his room and called to him.

"When can I get out of here, doc?" he asked.

"As long as it takes to heal those wounds," replied the doctor. "I can't give you a timetable."

That wasn't what Finn wanted to hear. He didn't know it, but he wouldn't leave the hospital until Christmas Eve.

"...WE WILL GAIN THE INEVITABLE TRIUMPH—SO HELP US GOD"

10

Franklin Delano Roosevelt

The House chambers seemed to overflow with congressional members, cabinet members, Supreme Court justices, and invited guests. The president's limo pulled up under the south entrance of the Capitol, where Secret Service agents helped him into his wheelchair. Roosevelt preferred to avoid being publicly seen or photographed in his wheelchair or even standing with his leg braces. Once inside, he waited in the Speaker of the House's office while people continued to file into the House chambers.

At 12:29 p.m. he heard a voice call out his introduction: "The President of the United States." Roosevelt made his entrance, thrusting his body forward on braced legs, assisted by his son James. The audience erupted with thunderous applause. Roosevelt mounted the podium and opened his notebook. Inside, his speech was written on special paper that wouldn't rustle as he turned the pages.

"To the Congress of the United States," he began. "Yesterday, December 7, 1941—a date which will live in infamy—the United States of America was suddenly and deliberately attacked by naval and air forces of the Empire of Japan."

He spoke of the treachery of the Japanese, who were in negotiations with the United States when the sneak attack occurred. He talked in general terms, giving no specifics of the damage done or lives lost.

"As commander in chief of the Army and Navy I have directed that all measures be taken for our defense," Roosevelt continued. "Always will be remembered the character of the onslaught against us. No matter how long it may take us to overcome this premeditated invasion, the American people in their righteous might will win through to absolute victory ... With confidence in our armed forces—with the unbounding determination of our people—we will gain the inevitable triumph—so help us God."

He ended his speech with an urgent request. "I ask that the Congress declare that since the unprovoked and dastardly attack by Japan on Sunday, December 7, a state of war has existed between the United States and the Japanese Empire."

As he finished he saw the cheering audience rise in a standing ovation. His speech had lasted only 6 minutes and 30 seconds, but he felt satisfied with it. Both houses immediately prepared to vote. In the Senate the vote was 82–0 for war. The final vote in the House was 388–1. The sole dissenter was pacifist Jeannette Rankin of Montana, the first woman to be elected to Congress.

Speaker of the House Sam Rayburn announced the resolution and signed it at 3:14 p.m. It was then signed in the Senate at 3:25 p.m., and finally Roosevelt signed the resolution at 4:10 p.m. The war that Americans had watched from the sidelines for more than two years was now their war too.

A world war.

John Garcia

John Garcia was finally going home. After three days of working around the clock to free men trapped inside the battleship USS *West Virginia*, he was allowed to leave. He'd be back soon. The work was ongoing. The men hadn't been released from the ship yet, and wouldn't for days, maybe weeks. In the meantime, Garcia would see his grandmother and, best of all, his girlfriend.

When he got to his door, his grandmother was waiting for him with a hug. But her eyes looked strangely sad.

"Aren't you happy to see me?" he asked her with a grin.

"Of course, John," she replied. "But I have some bad news for you. Very bad."

What could be worse than the destruction he had already seen—sunken battleships, dead men floating in the harbor?

"What is it, Grandma?" he asked.

And that's when she told him that his girlfriend was among the dead, killed in her house by a bomb. It happened that dreadful morning as she was getting ready for church.

As Garcia wept in his grandmother's arms he thought of the irony of it. He had been in the harbor, in the center of the storm, and got through without a scratch. His girlfriend was safe at home when she was bombed. There was an even greater irony that Garcia would not know for some time. The bomb that killed his girlfriend was not dropped by a Japanese plane, but accidentally from an American one.

Elizabeth McIntosh

Sunday, December 14, Honolulu offices
of the *Star-Bulletin*, 10:30 a.m.

Elizabeth McIntosh paced nervously outside the office of her editor, Riley Allen. It had been several days since she had submitted her story about the aftermath of Pearl Harbor and its effect on women. It hadn't appeared in the paper and she couldn't understand why. She had called Allen to find out why and now waited to see him. The door to his office opened. "Come in, Elizabeth," said Allen.

"Your story is great," he said, gesturing to the papers on his desk. "First-class job. You capture all the fear and concerns of the women of Honolulu. It's a truly compelling story, and I'm very sorry that we won't be publishing it."

McIntosh leaned forward, a puzzled expression on her face. Had she misheard him?

"You're not going to publish it?" she repeated, stunned.

"No and I'll tell you why," he said. "It's just too graphic, too honest. We're afraid it would be too upsetting for our readers at this sensitive time. I'm very sorry."

McIntosh lifted the pages from the desk and turned to the door. She could tell that Allen felt awful about it. "I'll be in touch for your next assignment," he said as she shuffled out the door.

She had written the best story of her life and no one would ever read it.

In its way, it was as strong a blow as the one she bore witness to a week before.

EPILOGUE

Japan inflicted great damage on the United States at Pearl Harbor, including the destruction of eight battleships and 188 airplanes. Some 2,403 Americans, including 68 civilians, were killed. One of the darkest days in American history also proved to be a turning point in World War II. On December 11, 1941, just days after the United States declared war on Japan, Nazi Germany and fascist Italy declared war on the United States. Congress responded with declarations of war against both countries the same day. The United States, despite its losses, emerged from the war stronger and more powerful than ever before.

President Roosevelt led the country in war, but he did not live to see its end. His death from a cerebral hemorrhage came less than a month before Germany surrendered unconditionally to the Allies (the United States, Great Britain, France, and the Soviet Union).

Japan fought on after the German surrender. Vice President Harry Truman became president after Roosevelt's death. As president, Truman approved

In reporting the attack, many newspapers used racist language
to refer to the Japanese.

the dropping of two atomic bombs on the Japanese cities of Hiroshima and Nagasaki. An estimated 200,000 people were killed or injured by the blasts— the only time nulcear bombs have ever been used in war. Japan surrendered a few days later on August 14, 1945, bringing World War II to a close.

Mitsuo Fuchida served Japan throughout World War II as a senior air commander. He led air attacks on the Dutch East Indies and British ships in the Indian Ocean in early 1942. He was aboard the *Akagi,* the same aircraft carrier used in the Pearl Harbor attack, at the Battle of Midway (June 4–7, 1942). Wounded in the fighting, Fuchida was rescued from the sinking *Akagi.* After recovering from his injuries, he served as the fleet air staff officer at the Battle of the Philippine Sea in June 1944.

Fuchida co-wrote a book about Midway in 1951 that was published in English four years later. By then, he had converted to Christianity and become a missionary. He worked to spread his religious message across the United States and Europe. "I would give anything to retract my actions at Pearl Harbor, but it is impossible," he wrote. "Instead, I now work at striking the death-blow to the basic hatred which infests the human heart and causes such tragedies." He died at age 73 on May 30, 1976.

Mitsuo Fuchida lived a peaceful life after World War II ended.

Samuel Fuqua's acts of heroism on and off the USS *Arizona* earned him the Medal of Honor. His citation read in part that he "supervised the rescue of these men in such an amazingly calm and cool manner and with such excellent judgment that it inspired everyone who saw him and undoubtedly resulted in the saving of many lives." Fuqua continued to serve in the Navy until July 1953. He died at age 87 on January 27, 1987.

For his courageous defense at Kaneohe Bay, John William Finn received the Medal of Honor on September 15, 1942. Of the 15 Medals of Honor awarded for the Pearl Harbor attack, Finn's was the only medal given for combat duty. The other 14 were given for rescue efforts.

Finn was promoted to lieutenant in 1943 and retired from active service in 1956. In 1958, he and his wife, Alice, moved to a 93-acre ranch in Pine Valley, California, where they raised cattle and horses and sold scrap metal. Alice died in 1998, but Finn lived to age 100, dying on May 27, 2010—the longest-living Medal of Honor recipient from Pearl Harbor.

Elizabeth McIntosh left Hawaii and returned to Washington, D.C., in 1942. She continued to work as a reporter, covering Eleanor Roosevelt and other government war stories. In 1943 she was recruited by the Office of Strategic Services (OSS). Fluent in Japanese, McIntosh was one of the few women who worked in the Morale Operations Branch of the OSS. She wrote propaganda, such as false news reports to be distributed to the Japanese to undermine morale.

McIntosh wrote about her experiences in a book, *Undercover Girl* (1947). In 1958 she joined the Central Intelligence Agency (CIA), the successor to the OSS, and worked there until she retired in 1973. She published another book, *Sisterhood of Spies* (1998), about the brave women she worked with in the OSS during the war. The rejected article she wrote for the *Honolulu Star-Bulletin* after Pearl Harbor was finally published by the *Washington Post* in 2012, 71 years after she wrote it.

A week after the attack, John Garcia was brought before a Navy court on charges of refusing an officer's order to go aboard the battleship USS *Pennsylvania*.

However, the charges against him were dismissed because he was not in the military and had saved the lives of numerous sailors. He returned to work cutting through the hull of the USS *West Virginia*. By the eighteenth day, about 300 men were found alive and freed from the battleship.

Garcia enlisted in the Army at age 17 and served in the South Pacific and the Philippines. After the war he worked as a police officer in Washington, D.C., and later managed apartment buildings in Los Angeles. As one of the youngest Pearl Harbor survivors, Garcia has been an active participant in Pearl Harbor events and anniversaries. His eyewitness account of the Pearl Harbor attack was recorded by writer Studs Terkel in his book of interviews with World War II veterans, *The Good War* (1984).

In the days after the attack, many of the dead were laid to rest.

TIMELINE

7:55 A.M.: A group of 182 Japanese warplanes, led by Flight Commander Mitsuo Fuchida, begins its attack on Pearl Harbor and the surrounding airfields on the island of Oahu, Hawaii.

8:10 A.M.: A Japanese bomb strikes the magazine on board the battleship USS *Arizona*, causing a massive explosion that kills most of the men on board and quickly sinks the burning ship.

8:15 A.M.: Chief Petty Officer John Finn begins single-handedly to fire back at the Japanese planes bombing the Kaneohe Bay Naval Air Station, 12 miles from Pearl Harbor.

8:17 A.M. (1:47 P.M. EST): Word of the attack reaches President Franklin Delano Roosevelt at the White House.

8:25 A.M.: The first wave of Japanese attacks ends.

8:30 A.M.: Journalist Elizabeth McIntosh arrives in downtown Honolulu, one of the first reporters to see the destruction there from the bombing.

8:45 A.M.: Sixteen-year-old pipe fitter John Garcia joins other young Hawaiians in rescuing sailors from the waters of Pearl Harbor.

8:57 A.M.: Aboard the *Arizona*, Lt. Commander Samuel Fuqua gives the order to abandon ship and heads for nearby Ford Island in a barge with a group of sailors on board.

9:00 A.M. (2:30 P.M. EST): Presidential Press Secretary Stephen Early delivers the first official announcement of the attack to the national news media.

9:25 A.M.: The survivors of the *Arizona*, led by Fuqua, arrive at Ford Island and are taken to a safe location by marines as the bombing continues.

9:45 A.M.: The second wave of attacks ends and the Japanese pilots fly back to their aircraft carriers.

11:25 A.M. (4:55 P.M. EST): President Roosevelt dictates his intended address to a joint session of Congress to his secretary Grace Tully.

1:00 P.M.: On board the aircraft carrier *Akagi*, Admiral Chuichi Nagumo decides against a third attack on Pearl Harbor and the carriers head back for Japan.

3:00 P.M. (8:30 P.M. EST): President Roosevelt meets with his cabinet to discuss the day's events. An hour later, he meets with congressional leaders.

DECEMBER 8, 1941

7:00 A.M. (12:30 P.M. EST): President Roosevelt delivers his address to both houses of Congress, seeking a declaration of war.

9:30 A.M.: John Garcia goes to work cutting through the hull of the battleship USS *West Virginia* to rescue crew members trapped inside the damaged vessel.

9:44 A.M. (3:14 P.M. EST): The House of Representatives passes the declaration of war against Japan by a vote of 388–1.

9:55 A.M. (3:25 P.M. EST): The Senate unanimously passes the declaration of war.

10:40 A.M. (4:10 P.M. EST): President Roosevelt signs the war declaration, and the United States has officially entered World War II.

11:00 A.M.: Elizabeth McIntosh begins to conduct interviews with the women of Honolulu for a story in the *Honolulu Star-Bulletin*.

SEPTEMBER 15, 1942: John Finn is awarded the Congressional Medal of Honor for his actions at Pearl Harbor.

APRIL 12, 1945: President Roosevelt dies of a cerebral hemorrhage, a month before the war ends in Europe.

AUGUST 15, 1945: Japan unconditionally surrenders, ending World War II.

GLOSSARY

barge (BARJ)—a large, flat-bottomed ship

bridge (BRIJ)—the control center of a ship

hangar (HANG-ur)—a large sheltered area where aircraft are parked and maintained

infamy (IN-fuh-mee)—a lasting, widespread, and deep-rooted evil reputation brought about by something criminal, shocking, or brutal

magazine (MAG-uh-zeen)—a room aboard a ship where ammunition and explosives are stored

morgue (MORG)—a place where dead bodies are kept at a hospital

negotiations (ni-GOH-shee-ay-shuns)—discussions in order to come to an agreement

ordnance (ORD-nahns)—military weapons, ammunition, and maintenance equipment

port (PORT)—the left side of a ship looking forward

portico (POR-ti-ko)—small porch with columns attached to a building

quarterdeck (KWOR-tuhr-dek)—part of the deck of a ship that runs from the midship area to the stern or rear

reconnaissance (ree-KAH-nuh-suhnss)—a mission to gather information about an enemy

starboard (STAR-burd)—the right side of a ship looking forward

turret (TUR-it)—a rotating structure on top of a military vehicle that holds a weapon

wardroom (WORD-room)—living and dining quarters for commissioned officers on a warship

CRITICAL THINKING USING THE COMMON CORE

1. Elizabeth McIntosh's story was not published after the Pearl Harbor attack because her editors felt it would be too demoralizing for their readers. Censorship in wartime happens all too often. Do you think it is necessary to limit freedom of speech in wartime? Why or why not? Support your answer using information from at least two other texts or valid Internet sources. (Integration of Knowledge and Ideas)

2. Some Japanese officials and soldiers, such as Mitsuo Fuchida, felt Japan would pay a high price for the sneak attack on Pearl Harbor. Why did the Japanese government do it, knowing the United States would retaliate? (Key Ideas and Details)

3. Before the attack on Pearl Harbor, many Americans were opposed to their nation getting involved in the war in Europe. After December 7, nearly all of these people supported the decision to go to war. What made them change their minds and could an argument still have been made to not go to war? Support your answer using information from at least two other texts or valid Internet sources.
(Integration of Knowledge and Ideas)

INTERNET SITES

FactHound offers a safe, fun way to find Internet sites related to this book. All of the sites on FactHound have been researched by our staff.

Here's all you do:
Visit www.facthound.com
Type in this code: 9781491470787

FactHound will fetch the best sites for you!

FURTHER READING

Raum, Elizabeth. *World War II Naval Forces: An Interactive History Adventure*. You Choose Books. North Mankato, Minn.: Capstone Press, 2013.

Stille, Mark. *Tora! Tora! Tora!: Pearl Harbor, 1941*. Long Island City, N.Y.: Osprey, 2011.

Tarshis, Lauren. *The Bombing of Pearl Harbor, 1941*. I Survived. New York: Scholastic, 2011.

Yomtov, Nelson. *The Attack on Pearl Harbor, December 7, 1941*. 24-Hour History. Chicago: Heinemann Library, 2014.

SELECTED BIBLIOGRAPHY

Arroyo, Ernest. *Pearl Harbor*. New York: MetroBooks, 2001.

Gillon, Steven M. *Pearl Harbor: FDR Leads the Nation into War*. New York: Basic Books, 2011.

Goldstein, Richard. "John Finn, Medal of Honor Winner, Dies at 100." *New York Times*. May 27, 2012. http://www.nytimes.com/2010/05/28/us/28finn.html?_r=1.

Goodwin, Doris Kearns. *No Ordinary Time: Franklin and Eleanor Roosevelt: The Home Front in World War II*. New York: Simon & Schuster, 1994.

Hillstrom, Laurie Collier. *The Attack on Pearl Harbor*. Detroit, Mich.: Omnigraphics, 2009.

"Interview with Elizabeth P. McIntosh and Frederick McIntosh." Veterans History Project. November 17, 2002. http://lcweb2.loc.gov/diglib/vhp/story/loc.natlib.afc2001001.30838/transcript?ID=sr0001.